# Biblical Storytelling In Youth Ministry

**Twelve-Year-Olds: Chosen and Blessed
Hoglah, Deborah, Samuel,
Jesus and Jairus' Daughter**

Ideas for Use in Youth Ministry,
Confirmation Class, and Spiritual Development
of Youth Using Biblical Storytelling

# Carol S. Wolf

**Fairway Press**
Lima, Ohio

BIBLICAL STORYTELLING IN YOUTH MINISTRY

FIRST EDITION
Copyright © 2009 by
Carol S. Wolf

Scripture quotations are from the New Revised Standard Version of the Bible, copyright 1989 by the Division of Christian Education of the National Council of the Churches of Christ in the USA. Used by permission.

Library of Congress Catalog Card Number: 2009924494

ISBN-13: 978-0-7880-2217-3
ISBN-10: 0-7880-2217-2

PRINTED IN USA

*To my husband and best friend, Dick,*
*for all his encouragement, understanding,*
*and support. We have been soulmates*
*since we were sixteen and seventeen.*
*I am so blessed.*

# Contents

# Introduction

My first encounter with the power of story was about thirty years ago. While teaching Sunday school, I realized I had missed whole sections of the Bible. I decided to read my Bible from the beginning, paying particular attention to the people and their stories.

I started with Adam and Eve and Cain and Abel. I soon discovered I had never heard much about Seth, their third son, yet his descendants included Enoch, who went to heaven without physically dying; Methuselah; and Noah. Isn't that often the way it is? The bad one is talked about constantly, the victim gets sainthood, and the steady one is forgotten or ignored. Then at the end of the census in Numbers, I found the story of Zelophehad and his five daughters. The Israelites were entering the promised land, and Moses was preparing to allocate the land. Zelophehad had died and his portion of the land would have gone to his brother because he had no male heir, but his five daughters asked Moses for his portion. Surprisingly, Moses takes their case to the Lord and the Lord says they are *right*, they should inherit their father's share. I had never heard that story before! Why? Was it because it was a story of children speaking up and asking for what was rightfully theirs? Was it because Moses gave women such respect? Was it because God gave these girls what was rightfully theirs, a decision that went against tradition?

The Lord saying they were right resonated so deeply with me that I began researching and reading whatever I could about this family and situation. Immersing myself in this story, I realized why it spoke to me. I had spoken up to my eighth-grade teacher when I was chosen to be editor of our school newspaper, and he told me the editor should be a boy and he was going to make that happen. As I shared this discovery with friends, I found them telling me their experiences and how they connected to this story.

I did finish reading the Bible after several years. Since then I have used these biblical stories in a variety of ways. Repeatedly, I saw and experienced something Margaret Wheatley said: "Telling our story and being listened to is one of the simplest ways to heal."[1] It is in the healing that we recognize the presence and gifts of God in these stories and how they relate to us today.

The power of story led me to the Network of Biblical Storytellers, an organization dedicated to encouraging people to learn and tell biblical stories. Each year since 1999, when I attend their Festival Gathering, I learn and experience this firsthand.

## Network of Biblical Storytellers

Their brochure indicates: "The Network of Biblical Storytellers was founded in 1977 by Tom Boomershine and Adam Bartholomew. Since that time the network has grown by thousands who have experienced biblical storytelling as listeners, tellers, and teachers around the country and around the world. They have celebrated over two decades of Festival Gatherings — several days of stories and laughter, centered on the Bible. We have gone 'high tech' by adding digital technology to support the telling of the word. NBS has also sponsored travel around the world, and storytelling workshops in countries all over the globe. To become more familiar with the mission, ministries, and the people of the Network of Biblical Storytellers, please visit our website at www.nbsint.org."

They have established the NBS Seminar that is a group of scholars and storytellers committed to academic support and performance criticism.

The Academy for Biblical Story-telling is a one-year certification program concentrating on telling and teaching skills.

8

There is also an optional second-year, Master's-level program that goes deeper, adds coaching, and requires the creation of an educational resource.

Not long ago I was reading an article about twelve being the age of spiritual accountability. It mentioned Jesus in the temple at twelve years old and several other children in scripture. I was looking for a theme for my Master's Project for the Academy of Biblical Storytellers. I began exploring the concept of twelve-year-olds in the Bible who were chosen and blessed and had an encounter with God. I chose the stories of Hoglah, Samuel, Deborah, Jesus, and Jarius' daughter.

Most faith traditions and cultures have a rite of passage from childhood to becoming an adult, which is generally about twelve years of age. Each faith tradition or culture marks this passage in different ways. A rite of passage, or coming of age, is a time when a person reaches a significant time in their life and it is celebrated in some form of ritual. The ceremony is unique, meaningful, and signifies that this person is becoming an adult and affirms membership in a community.

Prior to 1942, there was no term for a teenager. It wasn't until after World War II that the word "teenager" emerged and with it came an attitude of less responsibility.[2]

Until about 100 years ago, twelve-year-old boys were often doing heavy labor in apprenticeships and learning a trade. Girls were learning everything they could to take care of a home and family. Moral training and taking responsibilities seriously was a priority.

A new Search Institute analysis by the Center for Spiritual Development has discovered that early spirituality and religious participation is linked to later adolescent well-being. Their analysis finds that young people (in middle school) who describe spirituality as important, and who participate in a religious community, are better off, years later, in high school.[3]

"Spiritual development may be at a 'tipping point' for becoming a major theme in child and adolescent development. A growing number of scholars in various disciplines have invested themselves in this field. The public imagination appears to be ready in numerous cultures, traditions, and contexts, all of which are struggling with social changes that threaten to undermine the spiritual lives of young people."[4] Therefore, it is important for clergy and religious educators to effectively use those rites of passage that young children participate in for membership in their respective faith communities and for spiritual development. Included here is a brief overview of several rites of passage or coming-of-age ceremonies used by various faiths and cultures.

## Rites of Passage and Coming-of-Age Ceremonies

### Bar and Bat Mitzvah

In the Jewish tradition, a boy becomes a man on his thirteenth birthday after years of study. This is celebrated by a special service called a Bar Mitzvah (son of the law). He learns passages from the Torah that are read in the synagogue that day. This is the greatest day in the life of most young Jewish boys and continues today. They are then full members of the community.

The first Bat Mitzvah for girls happened in 1922. An American rabbi, Mordecai Kaplan, the founder of Reconstuctionist Judaism, believed that women should have full rights in Judaism. He had three daughters, so when his oldest daughter came of age, he created the Bat Mitzvah ceremony. Bat Mitzvahs are celebrated today in most synagogues.

## Baptism

Baptism had its roots in Judaism as part of the purification process. We know John baptized Jesus, and that practice has continued through the years. Baptism is a reenactment of Jesus' death and resurrection. It is practiced in a variety of ways, such as sprinkling or pouring of water or immersion. Many denominations baptize around the age of twelve, when the child can make the decision of following Christ for themselves. Some baptize infants and children, and then later confirm.

## Confirmation

Confirmation is another way of coming into the fellowship of the Christian church. The word "confirm" means to make stronger or firmer. Roman Catholic and some Protestant churches confirm young boys and girls as a renewal of their infant baptismal covenant. This usually occurs around twelve years of age.

## Vision Quest

In some Native American cultures, there is a vision quest as part of the rite of passage, similar to an initiation. Vision quest preparations involve a time of fasting and the guidance of a tribal medicine man. This quest usually occurs for the first time in the early teen years. The quest itself is a journey alone in the wilderness seeking personal growth and guidance from the Spirit.

Sunrise Ceremonial is an Apache girl's coming of age and takes place during the summer after a girl's first menstrual period, which usually occurs around the age of twelve. The ceremony lasts four days, during which time the girl takes on the role of Changing Woman, the first woman on earth and the mother of all Apache women.

## Islam

Islam has no specific rites for entering adulthood. Young boys do attend public prayers with the men, and girls will start to focus their activities more on the home and the family. During the month of Ramadan, both boys and girls will begin to undertake some days of fasting. As they grow older, the number of days will increase. When they become adults, they will be expected to participate in the entire month of the fast and only eat when the sun goes down.

## Africa

There are many cultures in Africa, each with unique customs. "Societies such as the Senulo of the Cote d'Ivoire teach young people the difference between knowledge and wisdom.... Wisdom involves human understanding and compassion, and promotes maturity and harmonious relationships.... The Senufo make statues in the form of a seated woman holding an adolescent. Called "Ancient Mother," she nourishes the young, uninitiated adult with the milk of wisdom."[5]

## This book is intended to help the leader of a group of youth or youth and adults

- Hear, learn, and tell the biblical story by memory. We will use the Network of Biblical Storytelling (NBS) process of learning the story by heart rather than just memorizing it. Then tell the story as it was originally intended to be heard. This allows each person to find meaning in places in the story that could surprise them. We should not be afraid to let our children think for themselves. Jesus said, "Let the children come to me, do not hinder them." What better way than to have children and adults hear, learn, and tell the biblical stories together.
- Experience the story in various ways.

- Explore the stories in scripture that relate to twelve-year-olds and their encounter with God.
- Find who they relate to in the story, then share how.
- Listen and learn from the stories of others.

Today we have an opportunity, as we gather in our faith communities, to live out the covenant that ties us to God and to one another. This means teaching and emphasizing to young people that God created the heavens and earth and that God invites us to share in this joy by hearing and learning the biblical stories in fresh, new ways. "The only way to start an exploration of the gospel as storytelling is to learn to tell the stories. Until you have experienced the stories as stories, all arguments about the meaningfulness of 'telling' the stories will be more or less meaningless abstractions."[6] In each of the stories in this book, we will experience how, when we become a part of the story, we often find meaning in places we never expected.

---

1. Margaret Wheatley, "No One Is Saved By Silence" (*Spirituality and Health*, Fall 2002), p. 22.

2. Online Etymology Dictionary, accessed 11/2/07.

3. Center for Spiritual Development — http://spiritualdevelopment-center.org, accessed 9/27/07.

4. Eugene C. Roehikepartain, Rev. Pamela Ebstyne King, Ph.D., and Linda M. Wagener, Ph.D, *The Handbook of Spiritual Development in Childhood and Adolescence* (Thousand Oaks, California: Sage Publications, 2006), p. 11.

5. "Africa: One Continent, Many Worlds, Coming of Age" Initiation Into African Society, www.nhm.org., accessed website 10/20/2007.

6. Tom Boomershine, *Story Journey: An Invitation to the Gospel as Storytelling,* (Nashville: Abingdon Press, 1988), p. 17.

# How To Use Each Chapter

Each chapter has five segments:

1. The scripture in a format that is easy to use for learning and telling and then using a different way to present it, *setting the stage.*
2. A monologue of one of the people in the scripture story based on various biblical and Apocryphal Old and New Testament manuscripts. These are surviving gospels and gospel fragments that have been discovered and published. Some are considered legends and are highly fanciful.[1]
3. An overview of the story and its possible meaning for today.
4. Personal reflections from the author — to whom in the story she relates and how there is a personal connection.
5. Questions for youth and adults to reflect upon.

My hope is that you will discover you are who you are today because of the people and the experiences, both good and bad, in your life. I hope, too, you will see how God is revealed to us in biblical stories, many of them about ordinary people, living in ordinary times, doing ordinary things, just like us.

We don't know exactly the emotions they would have been feeling or the words they would have been saying, but I wonder if we were there how we would have felt, what we would have said, and how we would have reacted. In each monologue I have imagined this.

We live in stories, and stories live in us. For some, experiences of dominance and repression lead to a fierce breaking out, but for others it creates a crushing pattern of destruction. Stories of forgiveness, truth, choices, friends, grieving, work, justice, prayer, and visions of the future can transform our own lives as well as the lives of others.

Let me introduce you to several of my "friends."

---

1. Edited by Wilhelm Scheelmelcher, *New Testament Apocrypha, Volumes One (1991) and Two (2003): Gospels and Related Writings* (Louisville, Kentucky: Westminster John Knox Press, 1991 and 2003).

# Chapter 1

# Hoglah — One of
# Zelophehad's Daughters

**Segment #1**
**The Scripture — Numbers 27:1-8**
Then the daughters of Zelophehad came forward.
    Zelophehad was son of Hepher, son of Gilead,
        son of Machir, son of Manasseh, son of Joseph,
            a member of the Manassite clans.
The names of his daughters were:
    Mahlah, Noah, Hoglah, Milcah, and Tirzah.
They stood before Moses, Eleazar the priest,
    the leaders, and all the congregation,
        at the entrance of the tent of meeting, and they said,
"Our father died in the wilderness;
    he was not among the company of those
        who gathered themselves together against the Lord
            in the company of Korah,
                but died for his own sin;
                and he had no sons.
Why should the name of our father
    be taken away from his clan
        because he had no son?
            Give to us a possession among our father's
            brothers."
Moses brought their case before the Lord
    and the Lord spoke to Moses, saying:
The daughters of Zelophehad are right
    in what they are saying,
        you shall indeed let them possess an inheritance

among their father's brothers and
pass the inheritance of their father on to them.
You shall also say to the Israelites,
"If a man dies, and has no son,
then you shall pass his inheritance
on to his daughter."

## Setting the Stage
(This process can be used with each of the scriptures.)

One of the best ways to learn the story is to tell the story back and forth with a partner. First, read one sentence or phrase at a time and then have the other person repeat it back. Then switch. Do this two or three times, then try telling it aloud to yourself and then to each other. "The two most important places in a story and in an episode are the beginning and the end.... By rethinking the words with the structure and verbal connections in mind, the story will quickly be stored in long-term memory and will never be forgotten."[1]

Invite one or two people to tell the story. Assure them they do not have to get it perfect and be ready to prompt them if needed. Encourage each person telling the story to be as dramatic or creative as they can.

## Segment #2
## Introduction to the Monologue

We know these five girls were Zelophehad's daughters and that he died before Moses assigned parcels of land to each man and his family. The meaning of each girl's name is Mahlah (sickness), Noah (comfort), Hoglah (boxer), Milcah (counsel), and Tirzah (pleasantness). I imagine, perhaps, that it was Hoglah who did the talking when they went to Moses to ask for their father's inheritance. We do not know how they felt or what they said to each other. The scripture records some of the words they spoke to Moses, and Moses' response to them and the people of Israel. Let's enter into one way this could have happened.

### Hoglah's Monologue (middle daughter of Zelophehad)

My name is Hoglah. I am the middle daughter of Zelophehad. You probably don't know me and maybe you have never even heard of me. I am not as famous as Sarah, who became the mother of our nation when she bore the child of God's promise, Isaac. I am not a heroine like our Queen Esther, who saved the lives of thousands of Jews. Yet, my name and my sisters' names are written in the pages of God's word. We did something no other woman in biblical history ever did. There were five of us all together. My youngest sister is Mahlah (whose name means sickness), then Noah (comfort), my two older sisters are Milcah (counsel), and Tirzah (pleasantness), and I am Hoglah (boxer) — and I am in the middle.

Perhaps to you, five sisters makes you think of pillow fights, hand-me-down clothes, and lots of giggles, but we were our father's greatest disappointment. He had five children but no son. Maybe to you that is not a serious matter. But you must understand my people. For my father, for any Jewish man, the greatest pride he could have is a son. The only thing worse, for a Jewish man, than having no son, was having no children at all. So my father hoped for a boy each time my mother gave birth. "A son, O God, please, this time let it be a son, five times hoping, five times a girl, another daughter."

Father told us how the Israelites had been looking for the promised land for forty years. During that time he became a father with no son. So you can see that he could have been angry with God. But he was not angry. He was a gentle man. He took care of his family. He taught us that God was good and just. He was a good father, especially after mother died, and he was faithful to God.

When God had us wander in the wilderness all those years, he remained faithful. Later, when a man named Korah gathered all the men against Moses and said Moses should not be our leader, my father did not join the rebellion. Then, when Moses found the promised land, our father died. Now what would we do? Because we were women we would have no land. Jewish law made no provision for a man's daughters to receive his inheritance, at least not until my sisters and I spoke up. It wasn't fair that only sons could inherit property. We are daughters, and it should be the same for us, too.

We talked and talked about what we should do. My sisters were afraid to say anything to Moses. Tirzah said that since she was fifteen, she would be marrying soon and she would take care of us. I said no, I may be only twelve but we have to do this for Father. They finally agreed, but said I had to talk since Mother and Father always called me Hoglah, the boxer. In the morning, after our prayers, we went to Moses and Eleazar, the priest. I was scared, but I remembered what Father taught us about God loving us and taking care of us. We did not want our father's name forgotten. We walked up to the tent of meeting and asked to talk to Moses and Eleazar. The families were already lining up to get their land. I was trembling when I saw so many people, but I couldn't let anyone know. No girl had ever asked for her father's inheritance. No one had ever dared.

Everyone was very quiet when I said we wanted to talk to both of them. Moses motioned for us to come forward. I felt the stares of people looking at my sisters and me. I saw the puzzled look on Eleazar's face as I told them our story.

Then Moses turned away. He didn't say anything. Was he ignoring our request? Was he thinking about it? Where was he going? Then he turned to us and said. "I will bring your case before the Lord."

We had to wait. Moses would seek an answer from Yahweh. My sisters and I would obey whatever God said. We would be faithful like our father Zelophehad.

When Moses returned, my sisters and I were still standing at the entrance of the tent of meeting. I searched Moses' face for the answer. Moses spoke to the whole crowd, "The Lord said the daughters of Zelophehad are right. They should receive their father's inheritance, and from now on whenever a man dies and does not have a son, his inheritance should be given to his daughters."

The joy and relief welled up in me as Moses spoke. My sisters hugged each other and cried. I stood still and looked at Moses. He smiled ever so slightly, and tears rolled down my cheeks. Forever after, our father would be remembered. Zelophehad was not a man without a son; he was the father of five daughters who had courage and changed the law of inheritance. Thanks be to God.

## Segment #3
### Overview of the Story

This short story tells us so much about this family and has an incredible message for us today.

Their father died just when they had found the promised land and all the property was being allocated to each man and his family. Early Jewish law stated that only men received land, and if a man died without a son his property went to his brothers. Daughters inherited nothing.

The girls had incredible courage to even think of asking Moses and the leaders for their father's share of the land and his inheritance. Zelophehad's daughters did not agree with the law saying only sons could inherit. I can imagine them trying to figure out what to do. Here were five sisters aged fifteen and under. We know that, since girls at that time were usually married by sixteen.

Then, they got up enough nerve to go not only before Moses, but Eleazar, the leaders, and the whole community (which consisted of several hundred thousand people) to ask for their father's inheritance. No one else had ever done that before.

Apparently Zelophehad had taught them that God was a glorious, good, and generous God, and that God listened and was just and fair. They learned their lessons well. Scared but determined, they asked and Moses listened. Incredible! How often do we seriously listen to children? Do we believe children have a valid point when they disagree with us? Do we even consider what they are saying?

That was 3,500 years ago. God changed the law of inheritance, and we hear God reinforce the original plan of creation, that everyone was created equal. Yet God's original intent, again, became distorted over the years.

This story has wider implications for us today than just the law of inheritance. It reminds us to have the courage to speak up against injustice in our world today.

Also, on the opposite side of the coin, as adults do we have respect and listen seriously to children or those that some consider the fringe people of society?

### Segment #4
### Personal Reflections

When I was twelve years old and in eighth grade I went to the first *middle* school in Buffalo. Four seventh and eighth grade schools came together in one building. At the new school, they started a newspaper as well as girls and boys basketball teams. I signed up for the newspaper and for the girls basketball team. The school paper advisors made me the editor. Then my homeroom teacher took me aside (this was 1953) and said I should not be the editor or play basketball. It was not ladylike and he felt I was a nice girl. A boy should be editor and I could do other things to help. I said, "No way!" He said he'd have to call my mother and have her come in.

My mother came in. After he explained everything to her, she told him I could do what I wanted. My mother, who was afraid of anyone in authority and would never speak up, spoke up for me. She did admonish me on the way home to not "get an attitude" toward the teacher.

That was a big step for my mom and I often wonder, "Would I be the person I am today if she had let him make me quit?" The rest of the story was that three months later, at Christmas, that teacher sent me a note saying I was doing a good job.

Hoglah's story has become my theme story as I work with adults and teens.


### Segment #5
### Questions and Reflections for Youth and Adults

1. Have you ever had a time when you disagreed and spoke up to an authority figure about something? What happened? Did they listen to you?


2. Were you right or wrong? Were you supported or not?


3. As an adult have you ever had a child or someone you consider unimportant disagree with you? If so, how did you react? What happened?

4. Do you speak up for the less fortunate or injustice today? Do you listen to others when they disagree with you?

---

1. Tom Boomershine, *Story Journey* (Nashville: Abingdon Press, 1988), p. 45.

# Chapter 2

# Deborah

### Segment #1
### The Scripture — Judges 4:1-16
The Israelites again did what was evil
  in the sight of the Lord, after Ehud died.
So the Lord sold them into the hand
  of King Jabin of Canaan,
    who reigned in Hazor;
      the commander of his army was Sisera,
        who lived in Harosheth-ha-goiim.
Then the Israelites cried out to the Lord for help;
  for he had nine hundred chariots of iron,
    and had oppressed the Israelites cruelly twenty years.
At that time Deborah, a prophetess,
  wife of Lappidoth, was judging Israel.
She used to sit under the palm of Deborah
  between Ramah and Bethel in the hill country of Ephraim;
    and the Israelites came up to her for judgment.
She sent and summoned Barak son of Abinoam
  from Kedesh in Naphtali,
    and said to him, "The Lord, the God of Israel,
      commands you, 'Go, take position at Mount
      Tabor,
        bringing ten thousand from the tribe of
        Naphtali
        and the tribe of Zebulun.
I will draw out Sisera, the general of Jabin's army,
  to meet you by the Wadi Kishon with his chariots and his
  troops;
    and I will give him into your hand.' "

Barak said to her, "If you will go with me, I will go;
but if you will not go with me, I will not go."
And she said, "I will surely go with you.
Nevertheless,
the road on which you are going will not lead to your
glory,
for the Lord will sell Sisera into the hand of a woman."
Then Deborah got up and went with Barak to Kedesh.
Barak summoned Zebulun and Naphtali to Kedesh,
and ten thousand warriors went up behind him;
and Deborah went up with him.
Now Heber the Kenite had separated from the other Kenites,
that is, the descendants of Hobab the father-in-law of
Moses,
and had encamped as far away as Elon-bezaanannim,
which is near Kedesh.
When Sisera was told that Barak
son of Abinoam had gone up to Mount Tabor,
Sisera called out all his chariots,
nine hundred chariots of iron,
and all the troops who were with him from
Harosheth-ha-goiim to the Wadi Kishon.
Then Deborah said to Barak,
"Up! For this is the day on which the Lord
has given Sisera into your hand.
The Lord is indeed going out before you."
So Barak went down from Mount Tabor with ten thousand
warriors following him.
And the Lord threw Sisera and all his chariots
and all his army into a panic before Barak;
Sisera got down from his chariot and fled away
on foot,
while Barak pursued the chariots
and the army to Harasheth-ha-goiim.

All the army of Sisera fell by the sword;
no one was left.

## Setting the Stage

**Talk show with embedded reporters**

Learn the story using the process in chapter 1. Then choose four people: one person to be the commander-in-charge, one person to act as talk show host, and two people to act as embedded reporters, one from Deborah and Barak's camp and one from Sisera's camp. Everyone else will be the audience. The needed props will be the map on page 27 (enlarged or redrawn on poster board) and a pointer.

**Talk show script**

**Host:** Welcome to the (name of your church or group) Talk Show. Today we have our Commander-in-Charge (person's name) to tell us what has happened the last few weeks with the war and our two embedded reporters, (name) from Sistera's camp and (name) from Deborah and Barak's camp.

First we will hear the details from our Commander-in-Charge.

**Commander-in-Charge:** *(tells the scripture story using the map to point out specific areas mentioned)*

**Host:** Thanks for bringing us up to date. Now let's hear what happened behind the scenes from our two reporters.

**Reporter #1:** *(using his or her imagination, tells what happened behind the scenes from Deborah and Barak's camp)*

**Reporter #2:** *(using his or her imagination, tells what happened behind the scenes in Sisera's camp)*

**Host:** Thanks very much for your insights. Now let's hear if our audience has any questions for anyone.

*(Host calls on persons in the audience with any questions. This can be as brief or as long as you choose.)*

**Host:** Thanks for joining us today. Tune in tomorrow for another interesting interview.

## Segment #2
### Introduction to the Monologue
We read all about Deborah in Judges 4 and 5. It was about 1125 BC, and Deborah was a prophetess and a judge recognized for her wisdom and insights. Barak is but a shadow beside her. Deborah's song is the song of a triumphant woman. It is from the song that we learn all about the battle. In the social environment of the day we can only imagine the unusual status she held. We also hear she trusted completely in God. I have imagined how I would have felt in her position.

**Deborah's Monologue**
My name is Deborah. You probably remember me from the Old Testament. I began feeling God's presence when I was very young. I always loved wandering on the hillside, listening for God's words. My father understood me and my desire to stay home with my family instead of getting married like most of my young friends.

You see, God talked to me and told me what he wanted me to do. As a young girl, when I sat under the palm tree near our home between Ramah and Bethel, some of our neighbors would come and sit and talk with me. They would ask my opinion of what they should do, and God always directed me what to tell them. After a while people started calling me a prophetess and a judge, and people came from great distances to seek counsel with me.

A few years later I met a wonderful man, Lappidoth, and we were married. He was a Philistine who had taken Yahweh as his God. Ours was a special love. He understood that Yahweh was my constant companion. There were more than a few nights when Lappidoth awoke to find me out on the hillside singing praises to God.

Through the years we wanted children, but we were never blessed with any. At first it was difficult to understand why. You see, for families in my time, it was thought to be a sign of God's disfavor to be childless. Yet, I had faith that it was God's choosing.

During these years Sisera, commander of King Jabin's armies, and his men continuously destroyed our vineyards and robbed our villages. Because of the awful things that were happening, people turned from God and started worshiping idols. Our life was becoming unbearable.

One night I awoke suddenly. Through our tent's curtain I could see the bright stars glittering. It seemed like the night called me. I got up and slipped outside, my heart pounded, I felt a strange tingling, and I was filled with joy. "I am here, God, I am Deborah."

Then I heard the voice. God asked me to speak to all the tribes and to declare war on King Jabin. I knew that it would not be easy. Many of my people would not accept being ordered about by a woman. It was going to be hard to convince everyone. Sisera, Jabin's commander, had 100,000 men and 900 iron chariots, and at most all we could gather would be about 10,000 men. At the next Feast of the Gathering, I went in front of the leaders. I told them what God had said, but they said they were afraid. "Nonsense," I told them, "we can get rid of these awful people, but we have to do it together and we must do it now."

"Who could lead our army?" they asked.

"Barak, he's the most capable and he lives close by in Kedesh." I have already sent for him. When he arrived, I told him, "Barak, the Lord God of Israel has commanded you to mobilize 10,000 men, lead them to Mount Tabor, and fight King Jabin's army." The Lord says, "I will draw your enemy to the Kishon River and you will defeat them there."

He looked dumbfounded. I watched him hesitate and look around. Uneasily, he said, "I'll go Deborah, but only if you go with me."

"All right," I told him, "I'll go with you, but I'm telling you now that the honor of conquering Sisera will go to a woman instead of you."

Barak gathered his 10,000 men and they went to Mount Tabor. I was there with the men and told them, "Now is the time for action, God is our ally." We all marched down Mount Tabor into battle not knowing what would happen. As promised, the Lord sent our enemies into a panic with a blinding rain and hailstorm. The Kishon River rose so fast that their chariots sank deep into the mud. Sisera got down from his chariot and escaped on foot. Barak and I followed the army to Harosheth-ha-goiim and they were all wiped out.

Later, when Barak went looking for Sisera he found the camp of Jael and Heber, the tentmakers. Jael came out from her tent and asked Barak what he wanted. He explained to her about the battle and that he was looking for Sisera. Jael invited Barak into her tent to see the body of Sisera, whom she had killed. God's prophecy was right again. A woman had killed Sisera.

After it was over, the people began to gather on the hill of Tabor. Barak and I stood before them and sang praises to God. After they left, I stayed on the hillside. I felt a chill go through my body as I again felt the presence of God. Then I heard the voice. I will never forget those words: "My peace I give unto thee, Deborah, for thou hast served me faithfully. No more shall ye fight. Peace, understanding, and wisdom, in my name thou shalt henceforth deliver these things to my people. I am God."

A blessed peace engulfed me. Praise be to the Lord and there was peace in our land for forty years.

## Segment #3
### Overview of the Story

This is another story of God believing a young girl had the wisdom and strength of character to lead an entire army. From her early years, Deborah welcomed God speaking to her. She listened attentively to God and responded to whatever she was asked to do. Many people came to her for advice.

As she grew up she followed her heart, and unlike the majority of women in those days she became a prophetess and a judge.

In the scriptures, she is one of the few women who is named before her husband, and her title is given. Her songs are the songs of a triumphant woman singing praises and giving glory to God.

When God spoke to her about going to war, she willingly accepted the position of co-leader of the army when Barak said he would only lead the army of 10,000 men if she went with him. She did, and they won the battle against staggering odds. Another woman, also, was responsible for killing Sisera, the commander of King Jabin's army.

This story reminds us to listen for God's leading and no matter how impossible the job seems, remember, "all things are possible with God," if we have wisdom and strength of character.

## Segment #4
## Personal Refections

I got married when I was eighteen years old. My husband, Dick, and I began helping the youth leaders in our church. Over the next few years plans were made to take a mission trip to Mexico City. We were asked to help chaperone. Dick and I agreed I would go, since I could easily take a vacation, but as a plumber summer was his busiest time.

Plans were well underway with fund-raisers, getting passports, and filling out forms. Then I discovered I was going to have a baby in March before the trip in August. Everyone assumed I would not go and leave a five-month-old baby.

Dick knew I felt God had inspired me to sign up for this mission trip and that I really wanted to go. We talked about it and he said to me, "Go. I can take care of our baby if my mom and your mom watch him while I work!" I told everyone I was going. Several people were upset with me, including my mother-in-law. They thought I was being irresponsible.

I went and it was the best thing that could have happened between us. When I returned Dick said, "I did it! I changed his diapers, fed him, played with him, and got up during the night when he cried." He was so proud of himself. That experience set the foundation for our marriage. It has always been a partnership and together we have tried to honor each other's callings from God. I am sure it is also one of the reasons he is so close to both our sons.

## Segment #5
## Questions and Reflections for Youth and Adults

1. Have you ever been in a situation where you felt God wanted you to do something that some would think inappropriate or impossible?

2. Did you do it or did you keep your thoughts to yourself and keep your mouth closed?

3. What happened? How did you feel?

# Chapter 3

# Samuel

**Segment #1**
**Scripture — 1 Samuel 3:1-11**

Now the boy Samuel was ministering to the Lord under Eli.
The word of the Lord was rare in those days;
visions were not widespread.
At that time Eli,
whose eyesight had begun to grow dim
so that he could not see,
was lying down in his room; the lamp of God had
not yet gone out,
and Samuel was lying down in the temple of the Lord,
where the ark of God was.
Then the Lord called, "Samuel! Samuel!"
and he said, "Here I am!"
and ran to Eli, and said,
"Here I am, for you called me."
But he said, "I did not call; lie down again."
So he went and lay down.
The Lord called again, "Samuel!"
Samuel got up and went to Eli, and said,
"Here I am, for you called me."
But he said, "I did not call, my son;
lie down again."
Now Samuel did not yet know the Lord,
and the word of the Lord had not yet been revealed to
him.
The Lord called Samuel again, a third time.
And he got up and went to Eli, and said,
"Here I am, for you called me."

Then Eli perceived that the Lord was calling the boy.
  Therefore Eli said to Samuel,
    "Go, lie down; and if he calls you,
      you shall say, 'Speak, Lord, for your servant is
      listening.' "
        So Samuel went and lay down in his place.
Now the Lord came and stood there,
  calling as before, "Samuel! Samuel!"
    And Samuel said, "Speak, for your servant is
    listening."
Then the Lord said to Samuel,
  "See, I am about to do something in Israel
    that will make both ears of anyone who hears of it
    tingle."

## Setting the Stage

Learn the story as before.

## Dramatic Presentation

Youth and adults are invited to take part in this interpretive process. The leader should encourage the participants to present their part seriously, dramatically, humorously, or whatever way they feel inclined to act out their part.

Choose four characters: Narrator, Lord, Samuel, and Eli. Have each character tell the story without using the scripture. Perhaps have several groups of four present and see how differently each group tells the story. If you have a large group you could invite four other volunteers to give it a try for different interpretations. This process helps everyone pay attention to what is happening in the story.

## Segment #2
### Introduction to the Monologue

We know some of the words Samuel said and we can feel his close relationship with Eli. His maturity is evident and yet we do not know what his relationship to his family was. We can only imagine how he might have felt. God called him by name and spoke directly to him. How many of us have heard God's voice, as Samuel did, and did not recognize it? How would we answer if we did know? Let's imagine how it might have been for Samuel.

### Samuel's Monologue

What a night it has been, to have God speak to me! Me! I have been living here in the temple with Eli, the priest, since I was a young boy, about eight or nine years now. I used to wonder why I did not live with Mother and Father like my brothers and sisters. Each year my parents would come here to Shiloh to offer the annual sacrifice. That's when Mother would spend time with me. She always brought me a new robe and would tell me stories of the family. She told me how she was married to Elkanah, my father, for many years, but because she had no children he took a second wife, Peninnah, who then had several children and often made fun of her. In the Jewish tradition, having no children was like God was mad at you.

Father was a farmer in Ephraim and went yearly to Shiloh for the annual sacrifice in the temple. He was a religious man who did all that the law commanded, but he did not understand the relationship between his two wives. When they went to Shiloh, Father would give Peninnah and her children meat and other food to eat, but he would give Hannah a double portion and would tell her it was because she had no children and he still loved her. Peninnah would get very mad and do mean things to Hannah.

Mother told me how one time she was so upset she came into this temple to pray and was praying so deeply to God to give her a son, and that if God did, she would give her son to serve the Lord all his life and not ever touch a razor to his head, which meant he would be a very special person. Eli saw her rocking back and forth and moving her lips with no sound coming out, and he thought she was drunk. So he hollered at her about being drunk in the temple. She told him she was pouring her soul out to God. Then Eli said to her, "Go in peace, and may the God of Israel grant you what you ask of him." It wasn't long after that she found out she was going to have a baby, and that baby was me. After I was born they named me Samuel. Mother said my name meant "appointed by God." My mother told me how when I was a few years old she brought me here to Eli to serve him and learn about God.

Eli told me how when my mother brought me here to live with him she said, "As surely as you live, my lord, I am the woman who stood here beside you praying to the Lord for a child, and the Lord has granted me what I asked of him. So now I give him to the Lord, for his whole life." Eli also told me how Hannah prayed a beautiful prayer.

It was the song she sang to me when I was little and each year when she came to see me. How could I ever forget? It is so beautiful. I often think of the beginning:

> The Lord has filled my heart with joy.
> How happy I am because of what he has done!
> I laugh at my enemies;
> How joyful I am because God has helped me!

I remember how Eli would bless Father and Mother, saying, "May the Lord give you children by this woman to take the place of the one she prayed for and gave to the Lord."

Well, the Lord was good to her, he gave her three more sons and two daughters.

Last night, when I heard my name called, I thought it was Eli calling to me again and again. I am so thankful that he figured out it must be the Lord calling me and that he told me what to say. This morning, when Eli asked me if God spoke to me and what he said, I didn't want to tell Eli everything God said. How do you tell someone you love that something sad was going to happen to his family? But Eli said to me, "Do not hide anything from me." So I told him everything. I told him that God would judge him and his sons harshly for the bad things his sons had done and he had not tried to stop them. I breathed a sigh of relief when Eli said, "He is the Lord, let him do what is good in his eyes." Eli told me the Lord had great things planned for me.

I promised God I would tell his word to all of Israel. My mother, Hannah, was obedient to God and kept her promise. I will be obedient and keep mine.

### Segment #3
### Overview of the Story

This story tells us that we are to keep listening for the call of God. In good times and bad times, when we are busy at work, when we are silent at night, and even when we are asleep. God not only calls people to work inside the walls of the church but outside of the church as well.

God may have to call us more than once to get our attention. God called Samuel three times before he responded and listened on the fourth time. With our busy lives and competing voices it may take a while to sort out God's call from others. The question is: Has God been calling you?

We also may need help from someone else to clarify the call. Samuel did not get it the first or second time and neither did Eli, but the third time Eli's experience helped him realize that it was probably God's voice speaking to Samuel. He told Samuel how to respond with willingness in order to move ahead.

God calls us by name and calls each of us differently. It might be a lightning bolt, a still small voice, or our own pain and brokenness. God has called through visions and dreams and even the persuasive words of others. No one is too young, too old, too small, too inexperienced, or too unimportant to be used by God for big, important work. In fact, the Bible is full of little people stories.

When we hear that call and discern its meaning, then we must begin on that journey. It is important to listen to those nagging ideas. What God desires us to do, God inspires us to do, and gives us the ability to complete the work.

### Segment #4
### Personal Reflections

Like Hannah, I made a promise to always be faithful. "Please, God, make my son well."

"A plastic bag taped to his side to urinate? But he's only five years old." I pleaded with the doctor, "Isn't there something else you can try?"

"We've tried everything possible, and with his last two operations being unsuccessful we have no choice," the doctor explained sadly. My husband and I left the hospital in a daze. At home we cried together and prayed.

For three years Kenny had been getting sicker and sicker. Two evenings prior to his surgery, Dick and I were sitting in our living room when the telephone rang. It was Pat, whom I'd known in high school. She and her husband, Jack, had recently moved to Boston, where he was doing his residency at one of the large hospitals. It all tumbled out amongst the tears, Kenny's illness, surgeries, and now this. Sympathetically, Pat asked if there was anything they could do. I answered, "I guess there's nothing anybody can do except pray." Three hours later the phone rang again. This time it was Jack. "Pat told me all about Kenny. I made a few phone calls, and if you can bring him up here in two days, I made an appointment for you with a pediatric urologist. He's the best in the country."

I couldn't believe my ears. "We'll be there," I said.

The next day we withdrew our consent for surgery and took Kenny home. We flew up to Boston with all his records, and he was examined by the doctor. "I can take care of this," he told us. "I have a new technique I'm using. I'll have him admitted in two weeks, and he'll be in the hospital for five weeks. Can you arrange that?"

"Absolutely," we said, "we'll be here."

Kenny had the surgery, did fantastically well, and he is now 44 years old. He has had an active life, played baseball and hockey, is healthy, and is now married and has an eleven-year-old daughter. I continue to struggle to be obedient to God and to respond to those inspirations that are given to me.


## Segment #5
### Questions and Reflections for Youth and Adults

1. Have you ever had a strong feeling you wanted to do something?
   a. Did you do it? What happened?
   b. Did you not do it? What happened?


2. Have you ever made a promise to God or anyone else?

3. Did you keep the promise? What happened?

4. Did you break the promise? What happened?

## Chapter 4

# Jesus In the Temple

**Segment #1**
**Scripture — Luke 2:41-52**
Now every year his parents went to Jerusalem
    for the festival of the Passover.
        And when he was twelve years old,
            they went up as usual for the festival.
When the festival was ended and they started to return,
    the boy Jesus stayed behind in Jerusalem,
        but his parents did not know it.
Assuming that he was in the group of travelers,
    they went a day's journey.
        Then they started to look for him
            among their relatives and friends.
When they did not find him,
    they returned to Jerusalem to search for him.
After three days they found him in the temple,
        sitting among the teachers,
            listening to them and asking them questions.
    And all who heard him were amazed
        at his understanding and his answers.
When his parents saw him
    they were astonished;
and his mother said to him,
    "Child, why have you treated us like this?
        Look, your father and I have been searching for you
           in great anxiety."
He said to them, "Why were you searching for me?
    Did you not know that I must be in my Father's house?"

But they did not understand what he said to them.
>    Then he went down with them and came to Nazareth,
>        and was obedient to them.
His mother treasured all these things in her heart.
>    And Jesus increased in wisdom and in years,
>        and in divine and human favor.

## Setting the Stage
Learn the story as before.

## Pantomime the Story
The leader invites someone to tell the story as others act it out, reminding everyone to fit their actions to the scripture story with convincing timing as the story is told. Characters needed are Mary, Joseph, Jesus, priests, teachers, and bystanders in the temple, along with relatives and friends on the journey. You might also want to have innkeepers answering doors and shaking their heads "no" during the three-day search.

## Segment #2
### Introduction to the Monologue
We know so very little about the child Jesus. We read about his birth, and then the scripture skips to Passover feast in Jerusalem when he is twelve years old. He remains behind in the temple with the rabbis. We see distraught parents and a calm child who is puzzled as to why they would be upset. He returns with them and is obedient to them. We hear nothing more for nearly twenty years. There are some legends of Jesus' childhood and infancy that are recorded in the New Testament Apocrypha. We have no idea what his life was like, but he was a boy that was learning what God had in his future. We can only wonder what his life was like with his family and friends. I have used excerpts from these legends.[1]

## Jesus' Monologue

I wanted to stay! It was the first time I really felt like I was where I belonged, in my Father's house. Talking with the rabbis and the elders in the synagogue, asking and answering questions, debating the Torah, and they didn't treat me like a child. Now I knew what my mother has been talking about. Now I understand the visions and the thoughts I have had for years.

But, my mother is right. I shouldn't have worried them like I did. I realize now that I have so much more to learn. It's beginning to all make sense. The stories I've heard, the things that have happened, the confusion and the fear. I knew I was different, but I didn't understand how or why.

I remember hearing the stories from my mother about my being born in Bethlehem in a stable with the animals all around. Mother said my father had to go to his hometown to register for the new tax that was decreed by Augustus, and my mother insisted on going with him even though everyone said she shouldn't because it was almost time for my birth.

One time I heard my mother and Grandma Anna talk about angels and shepherds and other things. When I asked my mother about them she said Yahweh had special plans for me and that I was the Son of God, even though I was their son, too. I didn't know what she meant. I did know that after I was born we had to go to Egypt because Herod had commanded that all the little boys were to be killed. What a terrible thing to do. They said he was worried a new king had been born that was going to take his place. Aunt Elizabeth was scared too and went into the mountains to hide my cousin, John.

I do know strange things have happened to me in the past several years. I remember playing with my friends and making clay shapes of birds and sparrows. One of the other boys' fathers had hollered at us that we shouldn't be doing this on the sabbath. I just waved my hand and the clay birds flew

45

away. Everyone was stunned, and he told people I was a sorcerer.

Once when my brother, James, was bitten by a poisonous snake, he was crying and some people were afraid he would die. I began to blow on the place where the snake had bitten him and he was instantly well. I remember the time our neighbor was splitting wood and hit his foot. He was bleeding badly and his foot was almost cut off. I ran and got some rags and reached down with my hands to stop the bleeding, and it just stopped bleeding. Just like that!

Oh, but one time my father was really bewildered. My friends and I were playing on the roof, and Zeno fell off and was lying on the ground. All the other boys ran away and left me there. They said to the crowd gathering that I pushed him off. Just then his parents arrived and looked up at me and accused me of being a troublemaker. I yelled down, "I did not push him off, he just fell. He wasn't being careful." So I leaped down from the roof, and I bent over him and shouted at him, "Zeno, get up and tell me, did I push you?"

Zeno got up immediately and said, "No, Lord, you didn't push me, you raised me up." Those who saw this were astonished, and Zeno's parents praised God for the miracle that had happened. They really treated me special after that.

Then, there were those conversations with my father in the carpentry shop. I thought he was talking in circles sometimes. He talked about how important it was for me to study the law and the Torah, and how I was young but there were things I needed to understand. He said he didn't understand everything but Yahweh was looking after me.

Quite honestly, sometimes these things have scared me. I know now that's why my parents rather insisted I spend time with the rabbis and teachers, even though I know I frustrated them with my questions and answers.

What a relief to finally feel I know my purpose. Now I must wait, continue to learn and keep these things in my heart, just as I know my mother does. I know I can always talk to her.

This time I am going to do what my parents say. I'm going to study the law, work in the carpentry shop, and try to discern what Yahweh wants me to do. I will wait and be patient until Yahweh says my time has come. Shalom.[2]


## Segment #3
## Overview of the Story

This story could be every parent's nightmare: to lose track of their child for days. They were frantically searching, and when the child was found they acted as if it was no big deal. This could also be every teenager's dream: to do exactly what they feel is important to them, at the moment, without consulting their parents.

Jesus' mother and earthly father were exceptional people, poor and humble as far as their culture and status was concerned. Mary and Joseph took Jesus with them to Jerusalem to the Passover celebration since he was now twelve years old and could be included in the activities in the temple. They must have trusted him and expected him to leave with everyone when the caravan was scheduled to depart. They were not concerned that he was not right by their side and in their sight.

Today most parents have fears for their children's safety, and unfortunately, rightly so. It is a challenge today for parents to find the right balance of trust and security.

Jesus, as a twelve-year-old, engaged in dialogue with the most learned Hebrew religious leaders. He must have felt affirmed and exhilarated to be listened to and respected. He was eagerly searching for knowledge. Our society today does not usually engage young people in intellectual conversations. Perhaps this scripture story is reinforcing that it is important to have religious conversation with young people and to strengthen our confirmation, baptism, and religious education classes. Ten-, eleven-, and twelve-year-olds are at an impressionable time in their development. What twelve-year-old wouldn't love to be taken seriously?

Jesus grew as a human being, his world and his faith expanded through a variety of people and experiences. Each of us has an opportunity to be a part of that learning process in the children around us.

### Segment #4
### Personal Reflections

When I was in high school, I loved English and writing. I knew I wanted to go to college and become a journalist and a writer.

My parents were not sure this was possible, since there were three girls and only one boy in our family and they felt it was most important for the boy to go to college. They had very limited money, so I was told I could not go to college. I would have to get a job and help the family out financially.

At first I was very angry. It wasn't fair. I was a good student and I even had a partial scholarship. After a while I got over the anger and disappointment.

When I graduated from high school, I got a job at the hospital I had been working at part-time. I worked in the business office and I loved it. Within the next year I married my high school sweetheart and we had two sons. We have had a great life together.

I never lost my love of writing. I have journaled, written stories, and through the years my employment consisted of writing job descriptions and a variety of other items. At church

I help with the newsletter and I have had a book, *Journey into Prayer*, published in 1995.

I realize now my parents were doing what they thought best, at the time, for the whole family. I learned that sometimes things do not go in exactly the direction you personally think they should. When those times occur it is important for each of us to discern the alternative path. Through the years I have always tried to figure out what was next and, through prayer, what was the best choice for me to make.

Four years ago, a new monthly newspaper, *After50*, began in our community. After reading it for three months, I felt it was a very positive and helpful newspaper for people over the age of fifty. However, there were no articles on faith or spirituality. After unsuccessfully trying to write a single article, I wrote them a proposal, that I be a monthly columnist for them and my column would be "21st Century Spirituality – Faith in Action" and each month I would highlight an organization that was serving the community out of their faith commitment and highlight the volunteers working there. I received a call two days later to come in for an interview and the answer was "yes," my dream of being a journalist was finally fulfilled. I laugh now and say, "I had to wait longer than Moses did for my promised land. It has been fifty years."

### Segment #5
### Questions and Reflections for Youth and Adults

1. How do you think Jesus' parents felt while they were searching three days for Jesus?

2. When they found him in the temple, how do you think they felt? Why do you think Jesus answered the way he did?

3. What was the problem from the parents' point of view?

4. What was the situation from Jesus' perspective?

5. As a result of this incident, what do you think changed in the relationship between Jesus and his parents?

6. How do you feel about the possibility that Jesus and his parents had the same struggles as most parents?

7. What are the struggles between you and your parents?

---

1. Edited by Robert J. Miller, *The Complete Gospels — Annotated Scholars Version*, "The Infancy Gospel of Thomas" — youthful years of Jesus (Sonoma, California: Polebridge Press, 1992, 1994), p. 371.

2. Edited by Wilhelm Schneemelcher, *New Testament Apocrypha, Volume One: Gospels and Related Writings* (Louisville, Kentucky: Westminster John Knox Press, 1991), pp. 439-446.

# Chapter 5

# Jairus' Daughter

### Segment #1
### Scripture — Mark 5:21-43
### (Luke 8:40-56; Matthew 9:18-26)

When Jesus had crossed again in the boat to the other side,
a great crowd gathered around him;
and he was by the sea.
Then one of the leaders of the synagogue named Jairus came and,
when he saw him, fell at his feet and begged him repeatedly,
"My little daughter is at the point of death.
Come and lay your hands on her,
so that she may be made well, and live."
So he went with him.
And a large crowd followed him and pressed in on him.
Now there was a woman who had been suffering from hemorrhages for twelve years.
She had endured much under many physicians,
and had spent all that she had;
and she was no better,
but rather grew worse.
She had heard about Jesus,
and came up behind him in the crowd and touched his cloak,
for she said, "If I but touch his clothes,
I will be made well."
Immediately her hemorrhage stopped;
and she felt in her body that she was healed of her disease.

Immediately aware that power had gone forth from him,
  Jesus turned about in the crowd and said,
    "Who touched my clothes?"
And his disciples said to him,
  "You see the crowd pressing in on you; how can you say,
    'Who touched me?' "
He looked all around to see who had done it.
  But the woman,
    knowing what had happened to her,
      came in fear and trembling,
        fell down before him,
          and told him the whole truth.
He said to her, "Daughter, your faith has made you well;
  go in peace,
    and be healed of your disease."
While he was still speaking,
  some people came from the leader's house to say,
    "Your daughter is dead.
      Why trouble the teacher any further?"
But overhearing what they said,
  Jesus said to the leader of the synagogue,
    "Do not fear, only believe."
He allowed no one to follow him except Peter, James, and
John, the brother of James.
  When they came to the house of the leader of the
  synagogue,
    he saw a commotion,
      people weeping and wailing loudly.
When he had entered, he said to them,
  "Why do you make a commotion and weep?
    The child is not dead but sleeping."
    And they laughed at him.
Then he put them all outside,
  and took the child's father and mother and those who were
  with him,

and went in where the child was.
He took her by the hand and said to her,
   "Talitha cum," which means,
      "Little girl, get up!"
And immediately the girl got up and began to walk about
(she was twelve years of age).
   At this they were overcome with amazement.
      He strictly ordered them that no one should know this,
         and told them to give her something to eat.

## Setting the Stage

Learn the story as before. Now choose a new setting for the story. It could be your own neighborhood, the old west, or the future; be creative. Act it out using the dialogue and words of the era. Have fun changing the setting.

## Segment #2
### Introduction to the Monologue

The story of Jairus and his daughter is told in Mark, Luke, and Matthew and yet the only thing we know about his daughter is that moment in time. This experience, I would imagine, had to have been life-changing for her. As a young girl I wonder what she thought of everything going on around her and the stories she heard afterward. If you or I were brought back to life as a twelve-year-old, can you imagine how our parents would react? Let's imagine her and her family and how Jesus brought a happy ending to a terrifying situation.

## Jairus' Daughter's Monologue

When I woke up and heard all the wailing and moaning, it really scared me. I thought people only did that when someone died. That man took my hand and said *"Talitha Cum,"* which means "little girl, get up" so I did. When I looked around the room I saw my mother and father at the foot of my bed hugging each other and crying. There were three other men standing there looking at me so bewildered. Then that man said, "Don't tell anyone what happened." What happened, I wondered? Then he turned to Mother and said to get me something to eat.

The next morning Mother told me the whole story. The last thing I remembered was being sick and lying in bed. Mother said I had been sick for weeks and weeks, and they thought I was going to die.

My father is Jairus, an important leader in the synagogue. Our family keeps all the Jewish laws. A year or so ago, he came home and started talking about this rabbi whose name was Jesus. He was so excited. He said Jesus was teaching and even healing people. Father said people thought he might be the Messiah and we had been waiting for the Messiah for a long time.

He said Jesus had made a blind man see. Can you imagine? Father said he had healed the sick and lots of people were following him. I also heard him say how some of the other leaders wanted to get rid of him. Father said they were scared of his powers.

Mother said when my father heard that Jesus was in town he ran to find him to bring him home to make me well. Mother said he knelt down and begged Jesus. I never thought my father would ever beg anyone to do anything; he is so important. Jesus said he would come to our house.

Mother said the whole crowd stopped when a woman who had been bleeding for twelve years touched his clothes. Now, Jesus would be unclean and could not come to our house. Mother said he talked to the woman and said her faith had made her well. No one really understood what he meant. She said our servants came and told my father and Jesus it was too late, that I had died! They thought I died! Jesus came anyway with those three men, his disciples Peter, James, and John. He told everyone else not to come with him. Mother said our neighbors and friends laughed at him when he came in and said I was sleeping and not dead, so he made everyone leave the house.

You know the rest of the story. The crazy part was that Jesus said we were to tell no one. But everyone knows, everyone is talking about it. Everyone is calling me Talitha.

I want to meet that woman. I want her to know I am okay. I don't want her to think I died because Jesus stopped to talk to her. I think they said her name was Veronica. I want her to know I am alive and we both have something in common. We both have a *new beginning* after twelve years, all because of Jesus.

## Segment #3
## Overview of the Story

This is a story that has several stories within it. One is Jairus, a leader in the synagogue, coming and kneeling before Jesus and begging him to heal his daughter. An important person bowing down to a carpenter's son, whom others in leadership thought was a rebel. Jairus was acknowledging Jesus' powers. A second is the woman who comes up behind Jesus and touches his clothes believing she would be healed. "In this story, however, it is a power claimed by a woman whose gender and status governed by socioreligious and cultural restrictions should have rendered her powerless."[1] She displays courage, and Jesus responds by confirming her healing and thereby giving her a new beginning. Friends and neighbors laugh at Jesus, saying she is asleep and not dead. Then Jesus taking her hand and telling her to get up. She does get up and walks around. She is twelve years old and now has her whole life ahead of her — a new beginning. We imagine that her life was very different after that. We imagine she continues to learn more about Jesus' teachings and perhaps becomes a supporter and maybe even a follower.

Over and over in our own lives we are given the opportunity for new beginnings. Some changes may be intentional and sometimes it may be an event that we have no control over. It is what we do with that opportunity that matters.

## Segment #4
### Personal Reflections

I remember one of my first new beginnings. I was eleven years old and was spending a week at church camp. My parents did not go to church, but there was a church in the neighborhood that was always inviting kids in the neighborhood to participate in everything. I started going there, and the church paid for every child that wanted to go to church camp. My parents agreed to let me go and I loved it.

I remember sitting around the campfire the last night and hearing our youth leader talk about committing our life to following Jesus as his disciples. I remember him talking about the blessings we had already received and that as Christians we are never alone. He told us stories of God, Jesus, and the Holy Spirit seeking out individuals for special service. We sang several camp songs: "Jacob's Ladder," "Standing In The Need Of Prayer," "Lord, I Want To Be A Christian," and "Spirit Of God." I still have the songbook. Then we were invited to throw into the fire a twig we had been given earlier as a symbol of our new beginning.

When we went back to church we were invited to join the baptismal class and be baptized by immersion when we finished the class. It was an experience I have never forgotten. Through my early teen years I was fortunate to have been nurtured by many people in that church. We moved when I was in high school, and I was led to another incredibly supportive church where my boyfriend joined me in participating in the youth group. He had never gone to church. When I invited him to attend with me, his comment was, "I will, as long as you never ask me to do anything." He also experienced the nurturing of our pastor and our congregational members both young and old. He was baptized six months before we married. It was a new beginning for us in many ways, and there have been many more along our journey.

I've learned to expect new beginnings oftentimes when I am not expecting them. Sometimes I respond willingly and sometimes I go into them kicking and wondering why this is happening to me.

### Segment #5
### Questions and Reflections for Youth and Adults

1. Have you ever had a time in your life when you felt you wanted to change something? Or a time perhaps you wished you could start something over?

2. What happened?

3. What part did your faith play in these stories?

4. How does this scripture story encourage you when you face a difficult situation or look at the opportunity for a new beginning?

1. Dennis E. Smith and Michael E. Williams, editors, *The Storyteller's Companion to the Bible*, Volume 13 (Nashville, Tennessee: Abingdon Press, 1999), p. 54.

# Conclusion

I hope you have enjoyed getting to know "my friends." I also hope you have gotten to know yourself better. Continue learning, exploring, and connecting the biblical stories to your own story. Don't stop here, continue your spiritual growth. If we open our hearts and minds, the biblical story enables us to make connections in our own lives that allow us to see how God was present.

What better way to continue your faith journey in life than reading the scripture stories and asking three simple questions: What is God doing? What are the people doing? What do we learn from this?

Blessings and joy on your journey!

# About the Author

Carol Wolf is a writer, speaker, storyteller, Associate Spiritual Director, and a leader of workshops and retreats.

Carol has worked as Executive Director of WNY Medical Network Services, Director of Development and Administrator of Highgate Medical Group, and Outpatient Department and Emergency Room Supervisor at Women and Children's Hospital in Buffalo, New York.

Carol has 35 years in providing leadership, direction, and administration of all aspects of medical practice management including financial, demographic studies, recruitment, and extensive interaction with employees, physicians, insurance companies, and business affiliates.

For ten years she was a partner and manager of Metcalf/ Wolf, Ltd., a medical property management company where she managed five medical office buildings.

Carol is currently a columnist for *After50*, a local newspaper, and a contributing writer for various publications. She co-hosts a television talk show for the Network of Religious Communities, is an Associate Spiritual Director at the St. Joseph Center for Spirituality in Clarence, New York, and chairs the Faith Based Initiative committee for the Center for Spirituality in Healthcare, SUNYAB, Buffalo.

She has just completed her master's degree in Biblical Storytelling and does performances and workshops.

Carol has been president of the Medical Group Managers Association, Buffalo Chapter, has been featured in the *Business First* newspaper, is past vice-president of Network of Religious Communities, and is the Network of Biblical Storytellers Annual Festival Gathering Coordinator.

Her workshop topics include:
- Stress Management,
- Motivation,
- Working Made Easier,
- Methods of Prayer,
- Angels,
- Meditation,
- Spiritual Gifts,
- Aging Well,

and many more.

Carol and Richard have been married fifty years and have two sons and four grandchildren.